The Training & Business Consultancy Ltd

MANAGING PEOPLE BETTER

PAMBO

a New Manager's Story

Follow Paul's journey
as he learns the hard way
how getting a promotion
may not be the easy ride
he hoped for.

Michael Baker
& James Davies

Managing People Better - PAMBO
A New Manager's Story

© 2013 Michael Baker and James Davies
© cover photograph of Michael Baker

Published in the United Kingdom by
The Training and Business Consultancy Ltd
www.thetbc.com
email enquiries to: PAMBO@thetbc.com

Paperback edition ISBN: 9781786153067
Ebook edition ISBN: 9781786153609

First Edition: November, 2013
Second Edition: October 2016
Category: Business / Performance Management

Managing People Better

PAMBO

A New Manager's Story

Michael Baker
& James Davies

Deb
best wishes
Michael

The Training and Business Consultancy Ltd

Foreword

If you have come this far you are either intrigued by the title or you are interested in managing your people better. Either way, indulge me for a moment as I give you the story behind PAMBO, and thank a few colleagues and friends in the process

Developing the concept behind PAMBO resulted from a particular frustration of mine. I was getting increasingly exasperated by the existing models on management which were old and clumsy. They used words that did not seem to fit modern business life and were based on research conducted before I was born.

I knew this frustration was shared by others who spent a great deal of their life training and developing people. My great friend Lyn Weimer and I shared many a story of how we would adapt a model so managers could relate to it better. I owe a great deal to Lyn. She has been a source of inspiration and courage to me over the twenty-plus years we have worked together.

In addition to businesses using out-dated ideas, I also experienced organisations spending a great deal of time and money preparing people to lead their organisation into a bright new future but at the same time the basics of good people management were being ignored. Managers were being trained and developed in great leadership ideas – however they were not focusing on the individuals in the company. They were failing to give regular and constructive one-to-one feedback to their employees.

Please don't misunderstand me, I work with a lot of great clients on leadership and executive development programmes, but we try to ensure that the basics of good people management are also in place.

My colleagues, in particular Ian Rothwell and Suzanne Unsworth, were instrumental in encouraging me to start developing the ideas around PAMBO and the follow-on model of instruction, information and influence. You will have to wait for the next book to fully understand that model. I'd like to thank them both for the encouragement, feedback and support – it meant a lot and still does.

The concepts for this book came together over a five year period. We researched it extensively with our clients and constantly tweaked it until we were completely satisfied that what we had was a good model of how to manage people.

Our clients have been amazingly supportive. Fiona Murtagh and the *Lloyds Bank* Learning and Development team gave us fantastic support as we played with an established business model developed by Professor John Purcell at the *University of Bath.* He in turn reintroduced an older model in his excellent study, *Unlocking the Black Box.* I had worked with John during my time at Bath, completing my MBA there in 1999. I am grateful to him for mentioning the model in his study and subsequent lectures. John and the team at *Lloyds* gave us the start we were looking for.

Going to a client and explaining that we have this new and updated idea around managing people, and suggesting that we can use it on the next programme, is a daunting task. But, without exception, each of them said "Yes, go ahead". They put a great deal of faith in the team at *The TBC*, in particular I would like to thank Andrew Jeremy and Sue Noakes at *Cunningham Lindsey*, Olga Toombs and the management team at the *Queens Club* and the whole Learning and Development team at *Rhondda Cynon Taff Council*.

In delivering countless management courses over the last twenty years I have drawn on a huge number of personal experiences of managing and being part of great teams. In particular, I would like to thank two of the best bosses I have ever had the pleasure of working for; Sam Squance at *AXA Shared Services* and Tim Dines at *Forte Hotels*. Both were amazing role models of how to get it right. I learnt a huge amount from them about human nature, listening, and always being yourself when trying to influence people. My only regret is that they were not my managers for longer.

The discipline needed to write and finish a book is never to be underestimated. I was massively encouraged by my mentor, Matt Pearce. He was a great and humble leader, and I count myself so lucky to have known and worked with him. He has helped much more than he could ever imagine.

A special word of thanks is also due to Ed

Barnett, my friend, business partner and all round inspiration to get off my butt and make things happen. He has created something very special at *Cartridge Mate* and my role was to support and encourage his great leadership. A big thank you to the team at *Cartridge Mate* (Kieran, Jamie, Dan and Chris), I love working with them. They make me laugh, feel proud and above all inspire me to keep working hard to help as many people as I can.

A final thank you to James Davies, my colleague and friend. James is a very hard working young manager who has a great ability to express himself. The story line in this book is his – I just added the management model. I hope James has learnt a lot about people by helping to create this book. It has been a total pleasure to work with him. I look forward to working with him on the second book.

So that's it, the story of PAMBO in brief, now enjoy the book – the story of Paul a slightly incompetent manager who discovers how to do it right.

Michael

November 2013
Michael.Baker@thetbc.com

1

On the eve of his twenty-eighth birthday, Paul Fowler was happy.

He was content.

Paul regularly made his daily commute from Cardiff to Bristol on the 7:00am train from Cardiff Central. He arrived at Bristol Temple Meads at 7:51am and had a six-minute walk to his office.

The commute allowed Paul to reflect on his life. He thought frequently about his parents, his wife Sally and, most commonly, his job. He was happy in his job, although he had gone through some testing times.

Paul graduated from the *University of West of England (UWE)* in 2006 with a degree in Business Management. After he graduated, he got a job with *IVEX*, a contact management company with offices across the UK. Specialising in outsourced telesales, they sell anything from insurance to advertising on behalf of their clients. *IVEX* are contracted by businesses that want to outsource their direct sales and canvassing.

When Paul questioned his career in contact management, he often thought about H.

One of the main reasons Paul was so content in his professional life was down to H.

It truly was.

Harold Jacobs, generally known as H was one of the Sales Directors at *IVEX*. He was Paul's boss. He was responsible for all sales activity across the West of England and South Wales.

H reported to the Managing Director, Ivan Brandenberg.

Brandenberg founded *IVEX* at the start of the millennium. He started in business in his early twenties, but was closer to sixty these days. Nobody quite knew his exact age.

Ivan was a burly man – a man of real charisma. You couldn't help but be intimidated by him, yet at the same time fall for his charm.

The team Paul worked in comprised of

himself, Linda, Harriet, Izzy, and Dylan.

Linda was 58, and had been at the company longer than Paul. In fact, she had been there longer than H. She was the person who challenged any new initiative or strategy, and often claimed that they "…had tried similar things years ago and it didn't work." She epitomised the phrase 'glass half empty'. Despite her pessimistic tendencies, Linda was a vital asset to the business. Her experience in a wide range of issues was absolutely invaluable.

Harriet and Dylan were two contrasting graduates who had only been with the company for ten months. They started on the same day and were very close friends. However, you couldn't find two more different people. They each provided different management challenges.

Harriet was the focussed one of the two. She was rigid in her manner and direct with her objections, very vocal, and often spoke out loud about the areas of her work she wanted to improve. In essence, she was the model employee. She always arrived early and left late, her attendance record was exemplary, and her manner towards all staff and customers was always courteous.

However, there was one statistic that let her

down – her sales. Harriet, for whatever reason, found it difficult to hit her targets consistently. Some months she was barely bringing in enough money to cover her own salary.

In complete contrast, Dylan was a sales machine.

Hitting targets was not an issue for Dylan, it was simply part of his working week. He regularly exceeded his weekly quota by Wednesday afternoon.

But his behaviour was appalling.

He regularly turned up late and was out of the door by 5pm sharp. He was not the most engaged of employees and it seemed that most of the time he did not want to be there. His heart wasn't in it. If it weren't for his sales figures, he would not have made it past the first pay day, he would have been long gone.

The final member of the sales team was Izzy. She was the one person Paul really cared for in the team. They had been to university together, they regularly went for drinks, and even shared each other's problems in work and at home – they had an unbreakable friendship.

That was Paul's team. That was his work. He thoroughly enjoyed his colleagues' company and although he spoke to his wife regularly about other opportunities, he could never bring himself to leave *IVEX*.

Paul was sipping his glass of Merlot, contemplating his twenty-eighth birthday. He wasn't overly bothered about getting a step closer to thirty, *"another step closer to retirement"* he optimistically assured himself. *"There was a time I thought thirty was old. There was a time I thought twenty-five was old."* He laughed out loud to himself at the thought. He had the house to himself, it was Sunday evening and Sally always visited her sister on Sunday evenings.

As Paul turned his attention to what he was going to have for dinner that night, his phone rang.

It was H.

He spoke words that Paul was not expecting to hear.

"Paul, I don't mean to alarm you, but from tomorrow there will be some changes in the office. The guys over in the East are on their knees and I've got to go and sort them out. I'm being seconded over to Cambridge for twelve months."

Paul nearly dropped the glass of red wine in his hand.

"What? What do you mean?"

"I'm calling to let you know that you'd better make sure you're wearing a damn nice suit tomorrow. We're creating a new role of Sales Team Manager and we would like you to take it. You're the new Sales Team Manager."

Paul froze. He wasn't hungry anymore.

He had been promoted. This did not happen every day. Paul was speechless.

Paul Fowler did not adapt well to change.

2

Paul had never wanted to ask so many questions.

"You're the new Sales Team Manager."

No matter how many times he repeated it, it was still a shock.

Paul spoke with H for over an hour.

There were times when Paul had difficulty asserting himself with his colleagues when they were working as a team, let alone try to impose himself as their manager. However, he felt confident that he could lead and deliver results.

H spoke calmly to Paul and discussed the reasoning behind his promotion.

Paul was determined that the team he was to lead would respect him and ultimately reach their targets… resulting in his career progressing nicely.

H reassured Paul that he was on hand to discuss any issues, he would have his full support, and would be only a phone call away to lend a hand to deal with any pressing matters should he need him.

As Paul ended the phone call, and sat back down on his favourite chair in his lounge, he stopped thinking about his birthday and started reflecting on his seven years at *IVEX*.

He began thinking about how much he deserved this.

Paul was sure of most things in his life. He was sure he loved his wife, he was sure he loved football, and he was sure he intended to retire by the time he was fifty-five. Also, he was sure that he wanted this promotion. It was his time.

This promotion would see him report to the MD, Ivan Brandenberg, in the interim, and then to H on his return.

Paul winced at the thought of walking in tomorrow knowing H would not be there to talk to. But his excitement grew at the thought of managing his colleagues and his impending responsibility for a substantial element of the business. However, Paul was concerned about his own ability to manage the team that he had, until now, been a part of.

If, Linda, Harriet, Izzy, and Dylan lost respect for him due to his mismanagement or poor leadership skills, it would devastate him. Paul was a likeable guy, and he liked to be liked.

Paul immediately thought of Izzy.

Izzy was Paul's closest friend, someone he confided in time and time again. How would he manage this relationship? That was his biggest concern.

She was a fantastic asset to the business, but she often complained to Paul about management and the way business was carried out. His worry was that if he became her boss, he would lose their friendship.

He worked alongside his team and heard them moan about *IVEX*. His fear was that every decision that he was going make would be analysed, scrutinised and subjected to similar moaning.

-o-

Monday morning came with an early wake-up call and a quick round of presents from his wife Sally.

Paul arrived at the office and immediately sensed the overwhelming tension.

"Everybody knew. They had to." Paul told himself.

However, as Paul arrived at his desk, the office was normal. The world was normal. "How *could* they know?"

It was 10:00am before anything happened.

Eve, the office HR Manager, came over to Paul looking flushed.

"Paul. The Senior Management Team are in the boardroom. All of them except H. They want to see you immediately." Eve's voice was quiet, yet assertive.

Paul entered the boardroom and voices hushed immediately. Eve stood beside him.

After what felt like an eternity, a voice came across the room.

"Ah Paul, please take a seat."

That voice belonged to Ivan Brandenberg, who sat at the head of the board table.

Alongside him was the Senior Management Team… minus H. Paul knew them all. The team comprised of the Financial Director, HR Director and Customer Service Director.

Brandenberg cleared his throat and spoke calmly. "Paul I'm going to make this quick. We've got a lot to get through. Have you heard about H?"

After a moment of hesitation, Paul replied "Yes. I have."

"Of course you have." barked Brandenberg immediately. "He would have given you the heads up. You don't have someone work for you for over ten years without getting to know their style. Paul, we would like to offer you the role of Sales Team Manager of the West Sales Department, with immediate effect."

Paul felt all eyes at the other end of the table narrow.

"So. Do you accept?" Brandenberg asked impatiently.

The Directors kept their eyes fixed on Paul. As if they were pressurising him into a sale.

"Paul, we have got an awful amount to get through this morning. Do you want the job or not?"

"Yes. I absolutely accept" responded Paul.

"Great" said Brandenberg. "If you could follow Eve, she'll take you over to her office to sort the paperwork out. We will be done here by 1pm. If we grab lunch together we can go

17

through my expectations, and any concerns you have. An announcement will be made at 2pm to the team."

Paul stood and looked at Eve. "Where did that come from?" asked Eve in a hushed voice as they walked back toward her office.

"This is mine. I've got this." came Paul's reply.

After half an hour or so of Paul and Eve going through his new job details, Paul went back to his desk to resume where he had left off. It was difficult to concentrate. He was so excited, he just wanted the announcement to be made *now*.

He wanted to pack up his desk. He was getting a new office. He was getting his own office. H's office.

He was thinking positively. Not only was he getting a new private office, but a salary increase, and extra holiday entitlement.

Paul started to wonder why he hadn't pushed for promotion years ago.

3

It was exactly one month since Paul had accepted the promotion, and it was going well. He had started in the role of Sales Team Manager with confidence, and he felt he was doing a great job.

He had not only settled in to his role overseeing the team but he was finding himself a dab hand at management… at least what Paul *thought* was management.

Several times throughout the month Paul was approached by one of his middle-management colleagues with a problem. Every time a problem occurred Paul acted swiftly and doused the fire then and there.

One Wednesday morning, Paul was in his

office going through emails when Chris Samuel came in. Chris was *IVEX's* IT Manager. He rarely acknowledged Paul, let alone came up to him to engage in conversation.

"Hi Paul. Sorry to bother you, but I've got a bit of an issue." Chris said rather sheepishly.

"Oh! No problem. Come and have a seat," replied Paul, still taken aback by his unusual behaviour.

"I've got a staff issue. Gareth is causing a bit of a stir. He doesn't quite understand how the new CRM software works. He's refusing to cooperate with the others and is creating a bit of a rift in the department. I'm not sure how to deal with it."

Paul immediately knew how to solve the problem.

"I know what we can do. I'll book him on a CRM software training course. I'll contact the company and set up the course for next week. Also, don't worry about Gareth's behaviour, I think he's being defensive because he doesn't want to look stupid in front of people."

Chris sat in his chair silently, as if he were expecting more. "Oh, right. Thanks for clearing that up Paul."

As Chris left the office rather bewildered,

Paul sat there feeling very smug with himself.

"This management lark isn't too difficult at all. It's just common sense." thought Paul.

Paul started to grow in confidence in a big way. Brandenberg was pleased with him, home life was on the up as he was bringing in more money, and Paul was happy in the knowledge that he was doing a good job. He was solving everybody's problems with relative ease. He couldn't be doing better.

As Paul finished for the day, he headed to the train station with a spring in his step. He thought of all those years he doubted his ability to make the step up. He laughed at how wrong he was.

He was a *brilliant* manager.

The train back home to Cardiff pulled up to the platform and Paul could see how busy it was. He was lucky if he got to sit down most nights. However, today was his lucky day. As soon as he walked onto the train he spotted a free seat amongst a crowd of standing passengers. They must have not spotted it. Paul didn't complain. He quickly sat down, waiting for something to go wrong. He waited for somebody to pipe up and say it was their seat, but nothing. This really *was* his day.

Paul couldn't contain his happiness. He had the biggest smile on his face and rested his head against the headrest and looked up at the carriage ceiling.

He was happy. Very happy. He couldn't remember the last time he had been this content with life. His mind started to wander off to his weekend plans when a voice came from in front of him.

"My, you look chipper for this time of day!"

The voice belonged to a middle-aged lady who was sat directly opposite. Her head was tilted to the side of her broadsheet newspaper. She was wearing a smile that rivalled Paul's.

"I've just had the best day." exclaimed Paul, who shocked himself with how upbeat his response was.

"Really? What have you done, won the lottery?" came her reply.

"Ha ha, not quite," he said, "it was just a good day at work."

The lady folded the broadsheet into her lap. "Tell me about it."

"Really, you want to know?" Paul was a little surprised at how interested she was.

"It's not every day somebody is this happy

at 6pm on a Wednesday," she said. She had a point.

"Well, I've recently been promoted."

"Oh! Congratulations!"

"Thank you. I was a little apprehensive, but now, I feel like I'm really starting to nail it!" beamed Paul.

"Wow. What is it that you do?" said the lady immediately.

"I'm the Sales Team Manager for the West at *IVEX*."

"I've heard of them. That's a pretty big company."

"It is. I've been there over seven years. I couldn't see myself working anywhere else." Paul was very surprised at this statement. He had never said that to anybody before, except Sally. He didn't really know it himself until he had just said it.

"So come on, tell me. What was so great about today?"

Paul explained to her about the way in which he handled Chris from IT. She sat there, quietly nodding along to everything he was saying. Paul was so enthused that he barely stopped to breathe.

He also explained how there was a problem with the Assistant Financial Controller, Judy.

"She came in all flustered. The petty cash for the month didn't balance and she couldn't see where she had gone wrong. I told her to go for lunch and, when she was out, I found the mistake and fixed it. I put the petty cash sheet back on her desk before she had even got back from lunch..."

The lady's face did not change expression the whole time Paul was talking at her.

"...and then Andrew, the Customer Relations Manager, knocked on my door and told me that he had heard that one of our biggest clients was on the verge of going with one of our competitors. So I rang their office and spoke with the MD to reassure him that we would work through the issue and that we really value them as a client. I even booked a meeting with him for next month."

"Next month?" she asked.

"Yeah. I couldn't do it sooner. I've got such a busy schedule and am off for a few days so it had to be next month."

"Right. So sounds like you *really* nailed it." she said in a questioning tone.

Paul was so energised that he completely

missed her tone.

"I know… right!" came his misguided reply.

With that, the train started to pull into Cardiff Central station and the occupants of the entire carriage started to make their way to the doors.

As Paul and the lady stood up, he looked at her and said "I'm sorry. I didn't even catch your name! I'm Paul."

"Jan," the lady replied. "I'll see you another time. Good luck with the new job."

"Thanks!" said Paul, enthusiastically, still unaware of her underlying tone.

-o-

Sitting in his office on a late Tuesday afternoon, Paul realised that since accepting the promotion he'd had very little contact with his team, in fact virtually none. He was so busy in meetings and getting to know his peers that he simply didn't have the time to catch up.

He was most concerned about not having contact with Izzy. He hadn't really stopped to talk to her about the promotion. He hadn't even stopped to talk to her at all.

Paul felt terrible.

"How selfish am I?" he asked himself.

Paul got up and walked across to his old unoccupied desk. Izzy's desk was next to it.

"Hi Iz," said Paul, nervously. 'How's things?"

Izzy's reply shocked Paul.

"So the Lord does mix with the plebs?!" she said sarcastically.

Paul looked back at her with not a clue what to say. Before he could say a word, Izzy spoke to Paul in a tone that he had not heard before. It was like they were only colleagues, not friends.

"Paul, just to let you know, I have formally applied for a job with *Connect*." Izzy spoke in a cold and unfamiliar manner that caught Paul off guard. *Connect* was a rival firm. The rival firm that Paul had turned down just two years previously.

"Oh! Right. What position have you applied for?" asked Paul gingerly.

"Sales Manager. I've sent them an application and I hope to have an interview in the next week or so," she replied.

Paul was stunned. He almost felt a sense of

betrayal. He looked at the floor and then again at Izzy.

"Good luck. Let me know if there is anything I can do."

Paul paused.

"Iz. Is everything ok? You seem sort of... distant."

People around them were leaving for the day. Paul checked his watch and it was 5:00pm already.

Izzy looked up at the clock and said "I've got to go. I've got a bus to catch."

Paul watched Izzy hurriedly get her things together and leave the office. His elated start to his new job had come crashing down to Earth.

As Paul went back to his office to collect his things, he noticed an email from Brandenberg.

The email asked Paul to compile his sales figures for the past two months, and projections for the next quarter, to present to the Senior Management Team at next month's meeting. Paul sent a quick email to Izzy and requested the figures on his desk in the morning.

"No problem boss." Paul whispered, as if Brandenberg could hear him.

Paul shut down his computer. Time to make the trip home. Another day done and dusted.

It was 10:30am when the sales figures were put on Paul's desk. He looked over them and nearly choked on his coffee. Paul sat there, speechless. He had the figures right in front of him. Sales were down, in a big way, and he had no idea why.

"How on Earth am I meant to give Brandenberg this!? He'll hit the roof."

Paul stayed in his office. This was the most frightened he had been in his professional life.

"If only H were here," Paul thought.

4

That morning felt like a lifetime. Paul still couldn't believe the sales figures. His eyes skated through the pages, repeatedly scanning the text and numbers. It was as if they were written in a language he couldn't comprehend.

He picked up his phone and called Izzy.

"Iz. These projected figures… are they correct?"

"Yes sir." came the chirpy response. Izzy seemed to enjoy telling Paul the news.

Paul didn't respond. He slowly put the phone receiver back on the handset, his hand holding on whilst he tried to process the enormity of what this meant to his career.

"I cannot give these figures to the Senior Management Team. How am I going to justify

this?" he thought.

This was a very different Paul. He could feel the sweat simmering on his forehead. He thought back to a few weeks earlier, his train journey with Jan. He had been so confident, so upbeat, so enthused with his new role. That seemed a long time ago.

Paul was angry that nobody had told him the projected sales figures were so low. He called an emergency meeting with his team. One by one, they filed into the office. Izzy's face bore a huge grin, and she was really starting to push Paul's buttons. He had never seen this side of her before. He decided to ignore it and get on with the meeting.

"Guys, projections are low. Really low. Does anyone want to let me in on why?"

The room was silent. Linda, Harriet, Izzy and Dylan looked at each other, then back at Paul.

Still nothing.

"C'mon guys. I need to know why our figures are so low!" Paul's voice got louder. "Is there anyone in this room that can explain to me why we are selling at an all time low. I need to know whose fault this is..."

"It's yours Paul" snapped Izzy.

Everybody looked at Izzy. She wasn't smiling anymore.

Paul was silent. He starred at Izzy, his face going red with anger. *"How dare she accuse me in front of everybody."* he thought.

"Me? My fault?" Paul questioned.

"I haven't had anything to do with the sales team in months..."

"Exactly!" cried Izzy. "Ever since you were promoted, you've barely spoken to any of us. You've been too preoccupied with your new office and your new responsibilities."

Paul didn't care for Izzy's tone – he was sure it was fuelled by jealousy.

"Izzy, you have no idea how much I have had to handle since taking this job. I haven't had the time to sit down with you all..."

He was cut short by Linda.

"It's your job to make time. It's your job to sit down with us. H always made time to sit down with us."

Paul had no answer. Linda was right.

"He did. He did make time for us." thought Paul.

Linda stood up. "Paul, we feel as if you've had no time for us since being promoted. We're working with one man down. You need to appoint a replacement now."

Paul looked at Izzy, her eyes darting between him and Linda.

"Guys. I'm sorry." Paul was looking at the floor. "I'll talk with Brandenberg and see if we can get the recruitment underway."

"It's not just that." said Linda. "You need to set one to one sessions. You're losing us… and we don't want to be lost."

Paul wasn't sure how to take that last sentence. It hurt.

There was a long silence. "I'm sorry guys. I don't want to lose you. This is serious. I need some time to think."

The four stood simultaneously and walked out with only Linda giving Paul a reassuring look. As Linda closed the door to Paul's office, he watched through the glass panels as the four of them walked over to the sales department. He was sure they were ripping him apart. He knew it.

Paul sat down, his neck pressing against the cold leather of the chair as he leant back and looked up to the ceiling. The phone rang and for a few seconds Paul wasn't going to answer it. He dragged his eyes away from the ceiling and saw the name of the caller. It was the Client Relations department.

"Yes?" Paul weakly sighed down the phone.

"It's Andrew. Did you speak with *Inspire*?"

Inspire was a financial planning firm that used *IVEX* to set up appointments with wealthy homeowners to review their wills, pensions and trusts. They were *IVEX's* biggest client in the West. Paul had worked on the account for over five years. Paul thought back to his conversation with Jan on the train. How he had diffused a recent rift with *Inspire*.

"I did." came Paul's confident reply. "I have a meeting booked with the MD next month as it goes."

"You do, do you?" Andrews question was rhetorical. Paul sensed something was up. "Paul, *Inspire* have cancelled the contract."

That last sentence crushed Paul.

There was silence for a few seconds.

"Paul? I've just received an email from the MD's PA. They've served us notice. In 30 days they will no longer be our client. What shall I do?"

"We've just lost our biggest client in the

region? Is this what you're telling me?" barked Paul, consumed by rage. "Remind me what your job is again Andrew? Aren't you supposed to be a Client Relationship Manager? Why have they cancelled?"

"They cancelled because sales were down. They cancelled because of *you*." he snipped back.

Paul couldn't believe what he had just heard.

"What do you mean they cancelled because of *me*?"

"The email said the MD was willing to work through the slump in sales and hear us out but didn't appreciate having to wait a month to see somebody. They're really hacked off."

Paul sprang to defend himself.

"That was the earliest I could see him!"

"Paul. It isn't your job to see clients. It's mine. I could have seen him immediately."

Paul's temper disappeared and was replaced with shame.

"I've been such a fool." He thought. Then he thought of H.

Paul picked up the phone and gave H a call.

H sensed all was not right. After a few minutes of Paul explaining what the problem was, H interrupted Paul.

"Paul, it seems like you're solving everyone's problems for them, your job is to help them solve their own problems."

He was right.

5

Paul somehow got himself through the rest of the day and, for the first time since taking the promotion, he actually counted down the seconds until he could leave.

As he sluggishly left the office for the train station, his mind raced with all the decisions he had made over the past two months and all the decisions he hadn't made.

As the doors to the train home opened, he took a free seat in the unusually empty carriage. Paul slumped into his seat, drawing a huge sigh as he ran his fingers through his thinning hair.

"Somebody's had a rough day." It was Jan, her eyes peering over her newspaper.

"You could say that." responded Paul unenthusiastically.

"What happened? Is it work?" asked Jan.

"What else?" sighed Paul.

"You were so upbeat the other week. What's changed?" Her face was smiling as if she were ready to hear all about his troubles.

Paul leaned forward and told Jan everything. He told her everything from Izzy undermining him, to *Inspire* leaving *IVEX*.

After a good fifteen minutes of moaning about his team, Jan cut Paul short. "How do you manage your people?"

"How do I manage my people?" repeated Paul. "Well, we have six-monthly appraisals and annual reviews – of course I haven't done them yet as I'm still quite new in the role..." Paul tailed off. He didn't even convince himself, let alone Jan.

"Do you know how I manage staff?" It was as if Jan knew he didn't know how to answer her question. She skated over his reply, as if she were saving him the embarrassment. "I use an idea that I developed over many years of managing people. I call it PAMBO."

"PAMBO? What does that mean?" asked Paul.

"It's a management model I use to consider the performance of a team member. It stands for

Performance equals *Ability* multiplied by *Motivation* multiplied by *Behaviour* multiplied by *Opportunity*, That's PAMBO."

Jan explained how a person's performance is equal to their ability; their motivation to apply that ability; their behaviour towards colleagues and customers; and the opportunity that we give them in the form of resources, equipment, feedback and involvement. As she spoke she wrote on some paper for Paul. *PAMBO* was written in huge letters on the page.

Jan leaned in, and said "Paul, what do you think your team is lacking at the moment?"

"Well, I'm not sure" came his reply, "I suppose they are lacking any sense of direction. They've all seemed a bit flat recently..."

"Right." replied Jan, breaking Paul off immediately, as if she knew he was on to something.

"So if a person is feeling rather flat and without direction, they're probably not enjoying their work. Would you agree?"

"Absolutely, Jan." said Paul.

Jan was on the edge of her seat. "So what are they lacking, Paul? When they get up for work in the morning, what is missing?"

"Their motivation," murmured Paul.

"Yes!"

"It's quite clear your team aren't happy with you. When was the last time you cared for them? When was the last time you spoke to them as people, or asked if everything was alright?"

Paul couldn't answer. He didn't need to. He looked at her and opened his mouth but, before he could muster a poor excuse, Jan leaned over and put her hand on his shoulder.

"Paul, the team is ticked off with you because you haven't loved them enough. They're annoyed at you because you haven't been there for them. You haven't been caring for them. It may seem silly, Paul, but they feel unloved."

Jan continued. "Before we get in to the specifics of PAMBO, you need to sort this out. What are you trying to achieve?"

"Well, I'm trying to get my sales back on target and my team back on my side."

Jan leaned in. "Tell me more."

"I guess I've neglected them. I've been a bit preoccupied with my peers."

"OK, so what ideas have you got to solve it?"

"Maybe I should arrange one-to-one

sessions and a team meeting? What do you think?"

"Do you think that will get your sales back?" she asked.

"I'm going to give it my best shot."

"So you're going to go and speak to them personally and professionally, then and only then, can we begin to use PAMBO. Once you've spoken with the team on an individual basis we'll start to look at ability – which is the first facet of PAMBO."

The train was pulling in to Cardiff Central station.

"I'll be on next Wednesday's train home. Come and find me in this carriage, and let me know how you get on. We'll make it a regular thing… once a week."

Jan gave Paul a reassuring pat on the arm as she got up.

"Thank you" shouted Paul as Jan strode off the train and through the crowds on the platform.

He had to speak with his team. He had to rebuild forgotten and neglected bridges before he began to think about their performance.

Paul felt a little better. Just a little.

41

PAUL'S PAMBO PAD

A person's PERFORMANCE
is equal to:

their ABILITY,

their MOTIVATION
to apply that Ability,

their BEHAVIOUR
towards colleagues, suppliers
and customers,

and the OPPORTUNITY
that we give them in the form of
resources, equipment, feedback
and involvement...

Performance = Ability x Motivation x Behaviour x Opportunity

6

As Paul entered the office the next day he immediately glanced over to the sales desks. Nobody was in yet. It was only 8:15am. No need to panic.

The first in was Harriet. Paul noticed she came in and greeted everyone with a beaming smile. You could not fault her enthusiasm. It was a trait that Paul had always admired. However, his concern was that her courteous nature was overshadowed by her inconsistent sales performance.

Linda soon followed and started her daily routine as the mother of the group – making a morning round of coffee and tea – while letting everyone know about her dreadful commute to work. She often exclaimed she needed to move jobs, something Paul doubted, considering she had threatened this on a weekly basis since he began at *IVEX* over seven years ago. Linda was, after all, reasonably set in her ways.

Izzy was next in, barely before 9am. Her timekeeping was never the best but she always made it in on time… just. However, her usual chirpy self wasn't the Izzy that *IVEX* had the pleasure of employing over the past few months. Paul could see from his office that she was in a bad mood and wasn't particularly happy in her job at the moment. This was a pressing issue for him, and for *IVEX*.

Paul had been sat judging Izzy's demeanour for a short while when he noticed Dylan hadn't arrived. He looked up at the clock in his office – it was 9:12am. This was typical Dylan, always late. Paul often wondered how long Dylan would last at *IVEX* if it weren't for his sales figures. Every month he either hit target or exceeded it – it was quite frustrating. His attitude to work and commitment to *IVEX* was best described as poor. He would often turn up late, sneak off early, and had a generally lackadaisical attitude to the working day.

Just as Paul was thinking about what to say to Dylan, in he came, strolling into the office with his headphones blaring – completely oblivious to the fact that he was nearly 15 minutes late.

Paul stood wondering whether he should say something – but then he realised he had enough enemies, and not enough friends in the team. He would revisit that issue another day should Dylan be late again. That was not the focus for today, today was about rebuilding bridges, not quashing them.

He needed to solve the sales problem.

Paul decided to act quickly. As he strode over to the sales desks, he found them all nattering amongst themselves. As he approached, their conversation stopped.

"Guys, can I have your attention for a minute?"

Harriet and Linda stopped what they were doing and looked up at him.

He clapped his hands together loudly "Dyl, can you stop for a minute. I need to speak to you."

Dylan took his headphones out of his ears and, as laid-back as his morning entrance, he slouched back in his chair and looked up at Paul.

Paul spoke.

"Thanks for yesterday guys. It was a much

needed wake up call. I really want us to sort this sales issue out and get our old team spirit back. Here's what I plan to do. I'm going to have individual one to one sessions with you today. These sessions will allow you to talk about what's gone on over the past couple of months, what concerns and issues you have and, most importantly, it'll give me a chance to listen to you... something I haven't done a lot of recently. Here are the times for our sessions." Paul handed out a timetable. Harriet was up first, followed by Dylan, then Linda and lastly Izzy.

"First thing tomorrow, we're going to have a team meeting to address the sales forecast and figure out how we get back on track. We've been through some testing times before, and I know we can get to where we need to be."

-o-

His one to one sessions proved invaluable.

He heard a lot of gripes from the team, mainly that he spent too much time with his peers and not enough time with them. He heard examples of where he took issues and solved them without their involvement. They felt he wasn't imparting any knowledge or providing lasting benefit, it was all about him.

He had a flashback to what H told him; *"Don't solve other people's problems, help them to solve their own."* To be a good manager he needed to help his team find their own solutions to problems.

Paul thought back to his session with Jan. She hadn't given him the solution, she had asked him simple questions about what he was trying to achieve and what ideas he had. From the one to ones it was clear he needed to do more of this. Paul needed to be a better manager – he needed to learn.

It was a testing day. It really was.

As he travelled home he looked forward to the next day's meeting with the team.

-o-

Friday afternoon was a period of reflection for Paul. Sat in his office contemplating the morning's team meeting, his phone rang.

It was H.

"How are you young man?"

H's familiar tones lifted Paul's spirits.

"I'm not going to lie – it's been a challenging week."

Paul went on to explain about the one to one sessions and the morning's team meeting.

"H, I feel positively better for it. There were times during the meeting I wanted to blurt out solutions but I didn't. I let them come up with their own answers while helping them on the way. Do you think I'm doing the right thing?"

"Absolutely. You're spot on. Remember, you need to be the Paul that was promoted, not the Paul that became a manager."

H was dead right.

PROBLEM SOLVING

Don't solve other people's problems,
help them to solve their own.

To be a good manager
I need to help my team solve
their own problems and
come up with their own solutions.

Performance = Ability x Motivation x Behaviour x Opportunity

7

Thank God it was Monday.

Paul had a whole list of wrongs to right. He started with one that he felt was of highest priority outside of the sales team – *Inspire*.

He called Andrew from Customer Relations.

"Andrew, that meeting with *Inspire*. I think we should go in together. What do you think?"

Andrew's stern reply came back, "Paul, if you think I'm going to be made to look like a fool in front of a client you can think again. You created this mess, you clean it up."

Paul spoke calmly "Andrew, this isn't about making you look like a fool. This is about team work. I want to go and apologise to *Inspire*, completely implicate myself, and then let you take the lead. I want to assure them that we really value them and that they should not cancel their contract. Let's face it, losing them would be a major headache for us both. You know that and I know that."

Andrew's response was far more welcoming. "You know what, that doesn't sound too bad at all. Let me know when the meeting is."

Paul put down the phone and felt a slight sense of achievement. One more bridge rebuilt.

Tuesday's meeting with *Inspire* and Andrew went well. Paul apologised profusely for the initial delay and any offence he may have caused.

He then shut up and let Andrew take the lead.

-o-

It was Wednesday. Jan day.

He couldn't wait to finish work to get the train home, to sit down with Jan and ask her a whole host of questions. The day whizzed by with Paul concentrating on the areas he needed to work on in order to help his team fulfil their potential.

Paul boarded the train as usual and there she was, smiling and waving enthusiastically to him. It was as if old friends were reunited. This was something he was not used to. He had friends of course, but none of whom were remotely interested in his work. Jan was different. She seemed not only to care, but actively encourage him to discuss his issues in detail.

"How are you?" asked Jan. Her smile beamed.

"Not bad at all Jan" replied Paul. "I've been looking forward to this all week. I've got a few things to run by you. It's to do with ability."

Jan leaned forward and whispered, "Go for it!"

"Well. What is it?" he asked, "I asked a few of my staff and they couldn't really define it. I was under the impression that ability was an innate characteristic that somebody either had, or didn't have."

There was silence. Paul looked at Jan hoping for a nod of the head. He didn't get one.

"Paul, you're not *completely* wrong. One aspect of ability is innate, but it is much more than that.", she continued, "Which skills are essential to make a good Telesales Executive at *IVEX*?"

Paul sat bolt upright from his slouched position.

"Right. OK. You need to be personable – especially over the phone. You have to be able to meet a frosty reception and turn it into a relaxed, yet professional, conversation. A confident manner is required – especially when you are asked questions. You are given a set script to stick to, but using your initiative and being creative with each call is encouraged. One of the things we look for when recruiting is creativity. *IVEX* does not want to be seen as just another telesales company, and likewise our calls do not want to feel as though they are just another sales call."

Paul was impressed by his own knowledge of what made a good telesales person. It was strange that he had never sat down and thought about what skills were needed to be successful in a role he knew so well.

Jan interrupted his reflection. "What else Paul? What knowledge do they require to perform well in the position?"

"Knowledge? Well, I guess knowledge of the CRM system we use, the telephone hardware, and computer software that we use to record data. Knowledge of using these systems allows the team to carry out their tasks well."

"And how do they acquire that knowledge Paul?" probed Jan – leaning closer to him as if he was on the verge of discovering a major answer he had longed to find.

"Through the training we provide them when they start and, I don't know, experience I guess…"

"That's it! Training and experience. So their ability is cultivated through the knowledge they have gained via the training you gave them, and the experience they get from a number of months and years in the role. Innate characteristics certainly contribute to a person's ability but they do not define, or more importantly, limit it."

Jan was making sense. Real sense.

She continued. "A person may be naturally personable on the phone, but lack the administrative skills to update their CRM database – thus compromising their ability in the role and having a less than perfect performance."

Paul sat back, reflectively.

"Now talk me through Harriet in terms of her ability. What parts of her job is she doing well, and what bits does she struggle with?"

Paul had no hesitation in replying. "Harriet is such a great person to have in the team. She's a diligent worker, an absolute perfectionist when it comes to punctuality and presentation, and she's the most reliable person I have had the pleasure to work with. However, she seems to come unstuck when making a sale. Her rapport with customers can appear to be too formal and she struggles to adopt a individual approach for each client, often coming across as delivering a rigid script. She doesn't give the customer enough of a great experience, and it's reflected in her sales..."

Jan stopped Paul in his tracks. "Paul, that's great." She began scribbling on a sheet of paper she had pulled from her bag. She handed him the piece of paper, with what looked like a table on it.

"Write down the people in your team across the top. In the left hand column write the different skills you need to be successful as a telesales executive. Just like you said to me. Then score each team member out of five on that specific skill. You'll then see who needs to work on what aspect of their skill-set, thus giving you an insight into who needs what training."

"That's a great way of looking at it Jan."

Paul sat and filled in the names of his team across the top.

"Don't fill it in now." said Jan. "Do it at work".

Paul was fairly content about the idea of ability now. He was keen to start using PAMBO on his staff and, now that he had the first piece of the jigsaw in place, he was getting excited.

"OK Jan, what about motivation?"

As soon as Paul mentioned motivation, the train manager came over the PA system announcing their imminent arrival at Cardiff Central.

"We'll have to leave it there until next week Paul."

"Have a think about motivation, but your primary focus should be on ability, and identifying where your staff need training."

With that, Jan bade Paul farewell, and he was left clutching the piece of paper with an overwhelming sense of confidence. He could start to understand his people better; he was beginning to understand how he could become a better manager.

	Linda	Harriett	Izzy	Dylan
Skills				
Knowledge				

ABILITY:

a person's SKILLS needed to
carry out the job effectively
combined with their KNOWLEDGE
of customers, products, procedures
and processes, and the industry.

Performance = Ability x Motivation x Behaviour x Opportunity

8

As Paul got into work and entered his office on a rain-soaked Thursday morning, his usual routine of switching his computer on and opening the blinds was forgotten. Instead, he took a sheet of paper from his briefcase and carefully placed it on his desk.

It was the piece of paper Jan had used to scribble the blank matrix on. He took his pad from his case and started replicating the grid. Paul thought back to what Jan had said.

He was to score the team out of 5 for each skill that is needed to be a great telesales person for *IVEX*. Paul filled in the sheet.

Skills	Linda	Harriett	Izzy	Dylan
Rapport Building				
Objection Handling				
Getting Past the Gatekeeper				
Closing a Deal				
Mental Arithmetic				
Written English				
Admin/Record Keeping				
IT Skills				
Knowledge				
Customers				
IVEX Products & Services				
IVEX Process, Procedures & Policies				
Industry				

He started off with Dylan. Dylan had clear strengths in rapport building and getting past the gatekeeper, so he gave him a 5 in each. His closing was pretty good, but could sometimes kill the sale by continuing to butter up the prospect, so he scored a 4. He was clearly a people person, however he lacked good administrative skills. His mental arithmetic was also weak, and his written English in emails was commonly found to contain misspelt words and poor grammar. He tended not to pay attention to the minor details. He was a true salesman and the world's worst administrator. Paul scored Dylan a mix of 2's and 3's on these aspects of ability.

Dylan's knowledge was better, he knew his customers well.

His memory was untouchable when it came to clients' names and preferences. He always remembered when they were going away on holiday, or when they had a special event coming up. His recall helped him to build rapport more than anything else. His fantastic memory made clients feel as though he was giving them a really personal service.

He was pretty good at blagging too. When asked about something he had little knowledge of – he had a knack of satisfying the client's question without really answering it. Paul scored Dylan a 3 for knowledge of products and services, 5 for knowledge of clients and 2 for knowledge of *IVEX*.

Paul moved on to Harriet. It was clear her

administrative skills and knowledge were high – so he scored her 4 and 5 on those abilities. However, he also knew where Harriet wouldn't score so well.

Paul was only able to score Harriet 2's and 3's on rapport building and unblocking, and had to give her just a 1 out of 5 for closing. That's where Harriet was really found wanting.

Linda was slightly more complex. Her skill sets hinged on her vast experience. Her written English and mental arithmetic were second to none. She didn't use a calculator and, as long as she had a pencil and paper, she could instantly work out a quote for a client.

Her rapport building, whilst not as personal as Dylan, was very effective. Her professional approach coupled with the fact she had been at *IVEX* for so long, gave her an infallible approach for client retention.

She often impressed the basics upon new starters, "if your admin is in order, then the rest will follow suit." Linda would often chastise Dylan for his laissez faire approach, and praise Harriet for her administrative strengths.

Her back-to-basics philosophy, while effective in terms of her performance, was also her Achilles' heel.

She was adamantly against learning new skills. She seemed almost scared of anything new, and her inability to move with the times, (and specifically with technology), resulted in wasted hours performing elementary tasks.

Linda would insist on posting documents to clients despite email PDFs being readily available on the *IVEX* server. She would often print documents and write on the paper when the document could be edited or completed on screen. She disliked using a phone headset, and often used the handset instead when making calls.

Linda's poor IT skills were a hindrance to the team, as other members (usually Harriet) would spend long periods talking her through simple tasks – thus wasting the valuable time of two members of staff in the process.

Paul sat and thought hard. He scored Linda 5 for the knowledge aspects of her ability, as she was a walking bank of information. Indeed, she scored highly on all of her abilities, bar IT skills.

Paul drew a long, deep breath.

Izzy.

There was still tension between the two friends. Paul hadn't managed to diffuse the friction that was evident between them.

Izzy was the most well-rounded member of the team. Her sales figures were reliable. She epitomised the word *consistent*.

Paul scored her 4's and 5's in most of her ability boxes. The only obvious area that needed training was *getting past the gatekeeper*. Izzy had a tendency to give up too easily if her target was proving tricky to talk to. She openly hated receptionists, and it was the focal point of a few humorous discussions in the office. The banter was one of the aspects of being in the team that Paul missed the most.

Paul recalled instances where Izzy had a frustrating call – trying to get past a receptionist who would not put her through to the relevant person. She would slap her hands on her forehead and run her fingers through her jet black curly hair shouting profanities... much to the shock of the rest of the office. He loved that about Izzy. She would always brighten up his day, even if it was at her own expense.

Paul sat back and looked at the piece of paper. It was clear now exactly what training was needed for each member of the team.

Paul spent a large part of Thursday afternoon and Friday morning having a further round of one to one meetings with each member of the team. They discussed areas for improvement and agreed to some actions to help bridge the gaps in their skills and knowledge. He was pleased he was starting to troubleshoot, and to attend to the issues that underpinned the team's performance.

Areas were identified for improvement.

Actions were agreed.

Sales and IT training needs were to be addressed by training courses and one to one coaching sessions. Paul would source books and other literature to help his team improve their knowledge. A team-building session would be organised to improve morale and team work.

The morale of the team was low. Very low.

Paul grew confident that training and team building would have a positive impact, but those issues were not going to magically disappear overnight just because he booked a few courses and coaching sessions.

It was a brisk Tuesday morning when his fears were confirmed.

Paul was sitting in his office trying to diarise an IT coaching session for Linda, when there was a knock at the door. It was Izzy.

Paul leapt to his feet to welcome Izzy, "Hi Iz! You OK?" It was the first time Izzy had made an effort to speak to Paul since he had been promoted.

"Paul, I need Friday off." said Izzy.

"OK, no problem," replied Paul.

"Great, thanks" said Izzy, as she turned away to walk back out the door.

"Going away are we?" Paul desperately wanted her to stay and talk. He missed their friendship dearly.

Izzy turned and fixed her shoulders towards Paul. She raised her head as if she were trying to compose a difficult reply.

"Swindon. I've got an interview."

Paul couldn't reply. The state of shock was so profound that Izzy easily read his expression, and left the office. He walked to the office window and placed his hands over his head, looking out at a busy Bristol city centre.

He had to act. Fast.

9

Paul knew that he had a crisis on his hands. If he lost Izzy, Brandenberg would have his head. *IVEX* prided itself on employee retention as much as client retention. Consistency and stability were core values. To lose a key member of his team was *not* what Paul needed.

As Paul boarded his train home, he caught Jan's eye immediately. He had lots to talk about.

"We have a problem, Jan." Paul slumped into his seat.

"I hope you had a good week too Paul..." said Jan sarcastically.

Paul felt awful. "Sorry Jan, I need to get something off my chest. I have analysed the team and scored them like we discussed. It's Izzy. She's having an interview on Friday. I really don't want her to leave."

Jan nodded sympathetically whilst holding her chin, analysing Paul's words.

Paul was awash with worry. "I thought we had covered motivation? How come Iz still wants to leave? I apologised for not being there as much as I should have. She can't leave, not now..."

Jan cut Paul off.

"You don't want her to leave? Is that as a friend, or as a manager, Paul?"

He wasn't sure about the answer. "Both... I think," he said rather tentatively.

Jan paused before speaking.

"Have you any indication as to why she may want to leave?"

"I know she was disappointed when I was promoted. I think she was jealous. We haven't spoken much since I took the manager job. She said I'd put my promotion before our friendship. I haven't ignored her, I've just been busy."

"How do you know she was jealous? Maybe she feels that you have no time for her." said Jan. "I think before you assume why she is leaving, you should try and establish the facts. In order to know why Izzy isn't happy, you have to know what motivates her."

"Motivates? Surely it's her pay at the end of the month. Do you think I should offer her more money?" he exclaimed, as if he had just solved a longstanding riddle.

"Not everyone is motivated by money Paul." said Jan, narrowing her eyes. "Some people are motivated by other factors."

"Like what?" asked Paul, laughing to himself.

"A number of things. How do you currently motivate your team?"

"There are several things we offer. If you hit your target by the end of the month then your commission on all monthly sales is increased from five per cent to nine per cent."

"Anything else?" said Jan.

"Well, if you hit your target by the 25th of the month you get a half day off, on the last working day of the month."

Jan pressed Paul.

"Anything else?"

"Actually, I've never had any reason to question the motivation of my team until recently," he said rather sheepishly.

"OK. So when you motivate people, what are trying to achieve?"

"I want highly engaged members of the team. I want a team that are hitting their targets.

"So is motivation for you all about hitting targets?"

"Yeah I guess it is. I want them to bring sales in."

Jan immediately crossed her arms.

"Well, Paul, if you have a problem to solve, and you get your team together to collate their ideas and suggestions, is that stopping them hitting their targets?"

Paul grimaced "Yeah. I want them to be committed, I want them to want to come to work and make a contribution to make the team better. So I guess it's broader than just targets."

Jan nodded.

"OK, so how would you do that?"

"Well, I would praise them when they're doing a good job."

"Yeah, praise is really important. It's vital that people have feedback to tell them they're doing a really great job. But motivation is far more than just reward and praise."

Paul struggled with this statement. "What else would motivate a person?"

"There are many reasons why someone is

motivated. Everyone is different."

"What do you mean?" he asked, bewildered.

Jan rolled her eyes. "Let me ask you, how do you get to know what motivates a person?"

"Well, I suppose you have to get to know them. You have to know what their circumstances are. I suppose if they are quite well off, money may not be the primary motivating factor." As the words came out of Paul's mouth, he started to unravel the perplexing question he had previously assumed was so simple.

"Would you ask them where they want to be in two years, or five years, or ten years?" asked Paul.

Jan leant forward "What assumption are you making, Paul?"

Paul paused for a second.

"That they're an aspirer?"

"Yes!" said Jan, smiling with relief as Paul's thinking was coming round to her line of thought. "You're assuming they want to aspire and progress. What if they don't? What if they are happy in their job and don't want to move? What does that tell you about the person?"

"That progression doesn't motivate them?"

Jan nodded. "So what would motivate them if they are happy in their current role and aren't looking to progress?"

"Security?" asked Paul – still unsure of his own words.

Jan smiled again. "Maybe! How would you find out what motivates them?"

"You'd ask them – wouldn't you?"

"What's the problem with that, Paul?"

He looked down at the floor "I suppose they may not know."

"Yep. It's a very direct question, and in my experience, it rarely works. You may have to ask subtle questions." said Jan.

Paul nodded.

"You would ask questions such as... how do I get the best out of you? Ask them about their high points, their low points, and what they think caused them. You can also use those questions to see how you've impacted on them as a manager. You will be able to recognise times when you've interfered and really upset them, causing them to lose confidence and ownership over an issue. You'll also see times when they're engaged and on fire, and that is a sight to behold."

Paul simply sat and looked at her.

"You know what? I had no idea motivation could have such a large number of variables. I just assumed it was bonuses and back-slapping."

Jan chuckled. "This is why these sessions are important. You need to understand your team as individuals on a personal and professional level before you can begin to analyse, measure and improve their performance. That's what PAMBO is all about. Paul, motivation is one tricky subject. It really is. To help you understand it I've produced this for you to take away."

It was an A4 sheet of paper – similar to the one Jan made to help him with the concept of ability.

With these words, the train came to a slow halt. The hour had gone by in a flash, as usual.

"Paul, before next week, you need to have a conversation with each member of the team, and really get to know what makes them tick, what makes them get up in the morning, and what drives them. Once you've had that conversation, you can begin to see how you can motivate them and get the best out of them."

"What about Izzy?" asked Paul.

"The only way to keep Izzy is to see what is bothering her now. It may be money, it may

75

be the role, it may be you. You won't know until you speak with her." With that, she got up and left the train.

Paul walked from the train station thinking about her parting words. *"It may be you."* Izzy might be leaving because of Paul.

That sent a shiver down his spine.

MOTIVATION:

is about being involved and committed to the success of the team and organisation.

It is about the contribution you make.

It's vital that people have feedback to tell them when they're doing a really great job and when things are not going as expected.

I have to get to know my team as individuals on a personal and professional level to help me understand their motivations.

I could ask my team questions like:

- "How do I get the best out of you"?
- "What am I doing that helps you do a great job"?
- "What am I doing that is getting in the way of you doing a great job"?
- "What are your high points and your low points, and what do you think causes them."?

Performance = Ability x Motivation x Behaviour x Opportunity

10

Paul knew that he desperately needed to speak with Izzy. So, on Thursday morning he asked Izzy what her plans were for lunch. The team usually ate out on Friday lunch time, but Paul had to act quickly. Izzy had an interview on Friday.

Friday lunch times were something of a team occasion and a real treat to round the week off. A treat Paul had missed dearly since his promotion. It was one of the reasons why Paul felt so distant from the team in spite of it being his fault. He had just got his priorities wrong.

He walked up to Izzy and placed a handful of leaflets on top of her keyboard. Izzy froze and looked up at Paul.

"Paul, what are you doing?" she asked in a

semi-annoyed, semi-curious tone.

Paul smiled.

Without letting Paul reply, Izzy demanded "What are these?"

"They're menus Iz. We're having lunch later. Just me and you. Like we used to do..."

She opened her mouth to reply, but Paul cut her off.

"You're not too busy, you haven't got other plans, and before you moan about money – it's on me."

Izzy looked up at Paul "I'm not going to that awful greasy spoon, Paul. You can take me somewhere decent."

Paul sensed Izzy was trying not to smile, but he couldn't hide his grin. He made eye contact with Izzy and, for the first time in months, he saw her smile at him in a way a friend would. After a momentary lapse, Izzy soon reverted to her cold, austere manner and accepted Paul's invitation for lunch.

Paul strolled back to his office feeling rather proud of himself. It was 10.30am and he had already broached the most difficult task of the day. 1pm couldn't come quickly enough.

But now it was time to speak to Linda.

Linda was the constant of the team. She had been there longer than Paul and Izzy put together. Linda was known for speaking her mind even if it was controversial.

Paul hesitantly went over to Linda's desk. She was in the middle of a call. Knowing her manner and fondness for procedure, Paul picked up a pen and wrote on her *Post-it* notes '3pm – my office?'

Linda looked up at Paul sternly. Profuse nodding was followed by the swift motion of her hand ushering him away. All this while she buttered up one of her best clients, assuring them of some key data she had obtained to help them on their campaign.

Paul strode back to his office and sat down.

Thinking deeply, Paul put himself in Izzy's shoes. He thought about his promotion and how he would have felt if Izzy had got it instead.

After a few hours of contemplating alternative scenarios, and getting on with some work, it was time for lunch.

Paul walked over to Izzy's desk. She stood waiting for Paul, desperately avoiding eye contact on his approach.

"Ready Iz?" said Paul.

"Yep. *Zino's*?" came the challenging reply.

"Brilliant," said Paul through gritted teeth.

He hated *Zino's*. Nobody knew this more than Izzy. It was the most overrated place in Bristol. Well, that's what Paul would tell anyone who'd listen.

It was Izzy's favourite, so Paul happily obliged. On the short walk to the restaurant Paul recalled Izzy and Harriet making cases for why it was so good.

"The food might not be great, but the atmosphere is superb and the staff are fantastic."

Paul replayed the answer he would always give "But why would you want to eat somewhere where the food was average?"

He could never understand why the team preferred *Zino's* over other restaurants in Bristol which had better quality food. Paul put it down to one of those things in life he would never understand. Like cricket.

After entering *Zino's* and ordering lunch, Paul decided to dive straight in.

"Iz, you know how sorry I am about not being there for you and the team over the past few months. I wanted to take this chance to speak to you about your role, and what I can do to make you happier and get you working at your best."

Izzy looked into Paul's eyes for the first time in months.

"Is this because of my interview tomorrow?"

Paul didn't want to lie.

"Well, I'll be honest with you Iz, that was the wake up call I needed. I want to keep you. *IVEX* needs to keep you. And I'll be damned if you leave because I wasn't doing my job properly, which I know I haven't been doing."

Izzy bore a poor attempt at a smile.

It was a start.

"Iz, tell me, how can I help you?"

She looked confused.

"Name one thing I could start doing to make you happier" he asked.

Izzy didn't hesitate with her reply.

"I've been at *IVEX* just as long as you Paul, and you know what, I'm bored. I'm *really* bored. You've had a promotion and you've been given the capacity to flourish. I haven't. I need to get out. The reason I've looked elsewhere for a job is that I feel as if I'm going nowhere at *IVEX*. I have no idea where my career progression is within the company, so I'm looking outside it."

He hadn't seen it. It dawned on him that she was right.

"Iz, go for your interview tomorrow. However, I want to have a brief talk with you Monday morning. I think you're right, and you need a role that you can progress in."

The rest of the lunch went well. Paul had his best chat with Izzy for a long time. An awfully long time.

As they finished their lunch and returned to the office, Paul sat and made notes. He wanted to write down the information while it was fresh in his mind. He knew Izzy had to leave her role, it was right.

However, he wasn't convinced *Connect* was the right fit.

It was time to speak to H about Izzy.

"Maybe she does need to leave?" Paul asked H.

"Paul, sometimes you need to let people go because it's right for them."

11

Paul's office clock gave the familiar double-beep as it did every hour, telling him it was exactly three o'clock. Within seconds, there was a knock at the door. It opened, and Linda stood there, politely waiting to be invited in.

This typified Linda. She epitomised professionalism and punctuality.

Paul invited her in, and turned away from his PC to give her his full attention.

"Linda, what keeps you here at *IVEX*?"

"I've never been motivated by money – you know that" she said in her usual calm and articulate voice.

"As long as I have enough money to pay the mortgage, run the car, go out for a few meals now and again, oh, and go abroad once a year –

I'm happy. I guess it gives me a sense of security with my lifestyle and future."

Paul said "Tell me more."

"Listen Paul, we both know that I'm not the best when it comes to change. Think back to our conversation about IT last week. I like things to be certain in life."

"So, how can I ensure that you are constantly feeling motivated and happy in your role?" asked Paul.

"Help me cope with uncertainty, and help me understand why things change. Don't try to change things without me understanding *why*."

"Great, I can do that. What else do you look for from work?"

"I ask for only three things from my workplace. One, I am paid fairly – which I feel I am. Two, that I am respected and treated professionally – again, which I feel I am. Three, that I have an amicable and constructive relationship with my boss."

Silence.

"Do you not feel we have an amicable relationship, Linda?" asked Paul, clearly surprised by her admission.

He waited for her confirmation that she did.

He looked at her.

"Paul, we *had* a very amicable relationship – I loved working with you as a colleague. As you well know, I haven't enjoyed the last few months of uncertainty with you not being around. However, I really like the fact that you've woken up and are making amends."

This was a shock to Paul. He never thought Linda would give him positive feedback.

"I have been at *IVEX* a lot longer than you Paul, and with the changes in the way we operate, especially over the last few years, I feel that standards have slipped. I can assure you that H wouldn't have let Dylan get away with his recent punctuality issues."

Paul knew she was right.

"It is incredibly frustrating to see him waltz in when things aren't going well, and for him to avoid any real consequences. It's a slap in the face to those of us who have worked here years… before he was even born. We've worked hard for this company and for the values it embodies. Don't let it all come undone because some young lad has poor timekeeping."

This made perfect sense to Paul. Of course Linda was frustrated.

He felt better for their conversation and

better because it was the end of the day, and almost the end of the week.

PAUL'S PAMBO PAD

MOTIVATION LIST

People might be motivated by:

- progression

- development

- security

- the relationship with their boss and colleagues

- being treated fairly and respected...

Performance = Ability x Motivation x Behaviour x Opportunity

12

Paul's weekly discussion with Jan had arrived. He had spoken with Dylan and Harriet regarding their motivation earlier in the week.

Dylan's had passed largely as he'd expected, but there was one surprise. He was motivated by money, however, Paul became aware that status and recognition were just as important. Dylan wanted the bells and whistles in life. He wanted the best business cards, the corner office, the flashiest car, and the title to go with it.

Harriet was also motivated by recognition. However, she wanted appreciation – not her name in lights. She longed for praise and plaudits to be heaped upon her. It was her constant striving for perfection, and the acknowledgment by others of her perfection that kept her motivated.

There were only a few minutes of pleasantries on the Wednesday evening train ride back to Cardiff.

Paul quickly got to telling Jan all about his meetings with Linda, Harriet, Izzy and Dylan.

Jan's response was frank.

"Paul, you have to play to each of their motivations. If Harriet needs praise, then give her all the encouragement and acknowledgement you can. If Dylan is motivated by money, offer financial incentives to draw the best from him."

"Well, I guess that leads nicely on to behaviour then." said Jan. "Tell me, what do you think I mean by behaviour?"

Paul sat back and thought about what Jan was asking. He was used to her asking questions that he had no answers to. Yet he still tried to answer them, usually resulting in him being so far away from the right answer that he embarrassed himself. Jan read his inability to answer quickly.

"What we're talking about here is an employee's behaviour when it comes to performance. If you went to a high street shop in the middle of town, and the person who served you on the till made little or no effort to engage with you, how would you feel?"

"Well, it wouldn't be great service, would it?"

"Absolutely," came Jan's reply. "If you were their boss, what would you say to them?"

Paul knew the answer to this one.

"I would say I want them to interact with the customers. Make eye contact, smile, be pleasant."

"Right! So their performance is not just about their ability and their motivation, it's also about them having the right behaviours. You cannot have an employee who works in customer service performing well if they are not polite and respectful to customers."

Jan continued. "Also, it's not just how they treat customers, and don't forget suppliers, it's how they interact internally. It's how they interact with their colleagues. Are they supportive? Do they contribute positively to the team dynamic? Do they help others when they are stuck?"

Paul nodded as Jan carried on.

"Perhaps they may be abrupt or even rude to those they work alongside. Those are the behaviours you need to identify when measuring performance."

Paul smiled.

This all made sense.

Of course his team needed to act professionally with customers and clients, but he had never thought that their behaviour towards each other would matter.

"That reminds me of last year," said Paul, "I was away with friends and we went for breakfast. The place we went to was spotlessly clean, the price was very reasonable and the food turned out to be just fantastic. However, when we ordered our food at the till, the man who served was awful. He made no eye contact and spoke in a very monotonous voice. There was no customer focus to his approach in the slightest."

Paul could feel himself getting angry as he recalled the story, much to Jan's amusement.

"To top it all off..." Paul's voice was steadily getting louder, "...when he gave us our change, he placed it on the counter! Not in our hands as we had done when giving him the money, but on the ruddy counter!"

"So, would you go back again?"

"Not in a million years!"

"Exactly! There are plenty of clean places that do good breakfasts – but the service is the clincher. It always wins customers over, and it always loses customers, when it's done badly. It is so critical. Tell me Paul, how should your team behave with each other?"

Paul, slightly less red-faced after cooling down from re-living his traumatic breakfast experience, said "Well, they should be helpful to each other, they should share ideas for improvement, and they should be understanding about the different ways they each like to work. Also, I guess they should have fun. We're only a small team so any conflict, no matter how insignificant, could be hugely detrimental to the team and their performance."

"Absolutely true! This aspect of performance can either make or break your team. Their behaviour towards each other is just as vital as it is towards your customers."

"You're right, Jan."

"Paul, we've had a great few weeks discussing ability and motivation, and you've done a great job in applying what you've learned. This week I want you to observe your teams' behaviour and the impact this is having on each other. Next week we'll talk about giving feedback to help people improve their behaviour."

PAMBO

As the train pulled into Cardiff, Paul knew it had been another hour well spent.

It was time to tackle behaviour.

PAUL'S PAMBO PAD

MOTIVATION is not just about money, although it helps! People might be motivated by:

- progression
- development
- security
- their relationships with their boss and colleagues
- being treated fairly and respected
- recognition and reward
- status...

BEHAVIOUR

Performance is not just about Ability and Motivation; it's also about having the right Behaviours.

I want my team to be polite and respectful to customers, suppliers and each other.

- are they supportive?
- do they contribute positively to the team?
- do they help each other when they are stuck?

Performance = Ability x Motivation x Behaviour x Opportunity

13

Thursday morning had a clear objective for Paul – observing the individual behaviours of his team.

He started with Linda. It was the obvious choice as she was always first in.

As Paul walked through the office and across the sales floor he noticed how she had already started to collect the dirty mugs that belonged to the others. She proceeded to take them to the kitchen, clean the previous day's tea and coffee stains from the inside of the mugs, and start to make fresh cups for the three imminent arrivals.

Paul had seen Linda do this countless times, and prior to his promotion he regularly came into the office to a piping hot cup of tea brewed just to his taste.

He stood in his office, slowly unpacking his briefcase with his eyes fixed on her. She was walking to and from the kitchen, carefully carrying mugs of tea. One after the other, a fresh cup was placed on Izzy's, then Harriet's and finally Dylan's desk, waiting for their arrival.

No sooner had Linda sat down, than Izzy and Harriet entered the office, engrossed in conversation. Paul wasn't sure what they were talking about but it seemed to involve a lot of laughing.

As they took off their coats, they both noticed their fresh tea steaming on their desks.

Izzy, wrapping her arms around a seated Linda, said "Ahh... thanks Linds, I was just thinking I could murder a cuppa."

"We genuinely don't know what we would do without our mum!" said Harriet.

Linda certainly took on a motherly role within the team. She would always remember birthdays, bring treats in to the office, and was always the first to distribute Christmas cards.

As Paul finished unpacking his briefcase he started to wonder where Dylan was. He checked his watch. Dylan was nearly ten minutes late.

This was not the first time Dylan had been late this month.

Dylan came strolling in a few minutes later.

Paul lost it.

He stood up from his chair, left his office and made his way over to the sales desks. Dylan had started to distract Harriet from her work, telling her about the crazy night he had last night.

"Dylan, can I see you in my office!" barked Paul – surprising himself by how annoyed he was.

Dylan followed Paul in to his office looking confused. "What is it?" he asked.

Initially, Paul struggled to meet Dylan's eyes. This was the colleague that Paul used to enjoy a Friday night drink with every once in a while.

Paul took a deep breath.

"Dylan you are late. Again."

"Oh I know, sorry about that. My bus was late."

"Then I suggest you get an earlier bus. I come from Cardiff and make it in on time. So does Izzy, Linda, Harriet, and so does everyone else in the company."

Dylan looked shocked by Paul's assertiveness.

Paul waited for a reaction from Dylan, but it didn't come.

"I suggest you rethink your priorities, Dylan." Paul pressed.

This time, Dylan did have an answer. "Priorities?! My sales figures have made this company a small fortune. That's something that can't be said for most of the team...'

Paul cut him off "Good sales figures do not make a good employee, Dyl. It isn't the be all and end all. You've got to pull your weight too. Your attitude is driving everyone nuts!"

Dylan stood looking at Paul, shocked at what his former colleague had just said. Paul could tell his pride had been dented. He told Dylan to go back to his desk and to get on with his calls. As Dylan left, Paul said "You'll be finishing at quarter past five tonight – seeing as you started at quarter past nine."

Dylan didn't respond but closed the door behind him and went and sat down at his desk.

Paul felt relieved, relieved that he had started to put Dylan in his place.

However, Paul couldn't help but feel that

he had an impossible task trying to manage the sales team whilst giving all four members his full attention.

The rest of his week was so full of target reviews and management meetings that he had very little time to communicate effectively with the team. Paul thought back to the conversation with Izzy about how he had no time for them, and she was right.

The weekend approached rapidly, as did Monday morning.

-o-

There was nothing better than a recharged sales team ready to hit the phones.

Paul always hated the first calls of the week as they tended to be the least fruitful. Most people were either in meetings or in no mood to be sold to.

For this reason Paul decided to hold team meetings every Monday at 9:15am. They were to discuss what each team member was working on during the coming week, and to review the previous weeks' figures. Also, it gave them a chance to address any team issues that came up during the previous week.

Paul noticed that Izzy was very sharp in her manner during the meeting and it wasn't just Paul who she was sharp with. Harriet asked Izzy a question about an account they both worked on, and the response she gave was notably stern. There was no need for it.

Harriet had asked Izzy a perfectly valid question regarding call volumes and Izzy responded in an incredibly defensive tone.

Paul made a note that this was something he should address.

The team got on with their calls just after 9:45am and Paul decided he would do something he hadn't done for a while – listen in on some of them.

He sat himself on a vacant desk in the IT area and plugged into the system.

He listened to Harriet first. She had struggled with sales in a big way, especially with objection handling and closing. It was an area they had identified for training a few weeks back, and he was interested to see how she had responded to the coaching she was getting.

He was stunned.

Harriet, with one of her calls, landed the sale – a very tasty sale. But it wasn't the fact Harriet had clinched the deal – far from it. She had battled with the gatekeeper to get through to her target. She didn't waver or dip in confidence… she was tenacious! She really wanted it.

Paul listened as Harriet had been given objection after objection and she handled them all in textbook fashion, but with the personalised flair that had been missing for large parts of her employment.

Paul could have wept with joy. The coaching he had organised was paying off.

Then he listened in on one of Linda's calls. When it came to handling difficult people, Linda was in her element. Paul heard one time where the recipient did not want to be contacted. She was an expert at diffusing difficult situations. In this case she calmly reassured the person that she would remove their contact information from *IVEX's* database.

The call ended with a friendly exchange and despite it resulting in no sale it was one potential customer who, instead of being annoyed at receiving a cold call, was pleased that they were listened to and that their demands were satisfied.

Paul reflected that if this was her normal behaviour, and he was sure it was, then customer service was in safe hands.

Paul made a note.

He had to tell her how great she was at doing that.

But how should he do it?

14

Paul dashed out of the door. He knew he couldn't be late. If only he hadn't taken that last call.

It was 5:10pm.

It was Wednesday.

It was time to see Jan.

So much had happened in the last week and Paul was bursting at the seams with examples of behaviours and stories that had come up since last Wednesday.

Most of all, Paul wanted to tell Jan how he had dealt with Dylan. He wanted to show her how much he had taken on board. It was as if he were a proud son – dying to show his mother his glowing school report.

Paul was running late. He had to be at

Bristol Temple Meads station for the 5:15pm train back to Cardiff. He could not miss it.

It normally took Paul six minutes to walk from the office to the station. This was going to be tight.

As he approached the train, he could see Jan in the farthest compartment. She was looking all around her, searching for him.

Paul ran.

He was less than 100 yards from the train. He could see the conductor checking his watch.

"WAIT!" Paul shouted.

50 yards.

The conductor placed his whistle in his mouth and gave a toot to let the driver know he could start the engine.

25 yards.

Paul was beginning to tire. He hadn't run properly in years.

10 yards.

Just as the conductor stepped inside the train Paul managed to jump through the closing doors – causing some alarm to the passengers within. He was on the train, and more importantly he could see Jan.

She sat there, speechless, as he made his

way over to see her. He was panting, sweating and generally not with it.

"Let me guess." said Jan with a wry smile across her face. "Not as fit as you once were?"

"No... not... really" he gasped.

It took Paul the best part of five minutes to get his breath back.

"I'll admit, I haven't exercised in a little while," laughed Paul.

Jan got down to business.

"Right, tell me how your week was."

Paul updated Jan about Izzy.

He told her about how he dealt with Dylan and his lateness.

Jan's face dropped.

"What you've told me raises loads of issues about a complicated individual. Let's go back to the basics about how we give feedback. Once you've got the basics right we'll go back and talk about Dylan. He's a complex character."

Paul leaned in, "Are you trying to politely tell me that I got it wrong?"

Ignoring Paul's question Jan said "I'm not too sure that was the best way to handle it. Let's start from the beginning."

Paul felt confused. He was so sure that he had done the right thing.

"I had to act. I couldn't let him swan in late every day. What message would that send out to the team?"

Jan said "I know, Paul. Absolutely. The important thing is that feedback is about helping people change their future performance. But wait a minute. I'm jumping ahead. Let's start from the beginning.

"When was the last time you gave any of your team feedback?"

Paul's blank expression told Jan all she needed to know.

"OK. How do you think you would go about giving feedback?"

Paul's blank expression did little to improve.

"I've heard about the sandwich technique. You tell somebody they're doing a good job, then give criticism, then leave them on a high. I guess that's how I would do it."

Jan flicked her hair back and rolled up her sleeves as if she was getting down to work.

"The sandwich technique has been around a while. I personally do not use it. I find it a bit patronising and a little old fashioned. Most people, when you start praising them, sense that a negative is about to come and brace themselves. I much prefer to treat people as adults."

"Wow! You really don't like it!" chuckled Paul.

"I guess not. When I give feedback I like to talk about specific examples – the impact their behaviour had, and the actions I want from them in the future."

Paul, nodding, said "That sounds pretty straight forward. Give me an example."

"When you make such a real effort to catch the train on a Wednesday night it makes me believe that you really value our sessions. Thank you. Please keep it up."

Paul smiled. "How do I apply this to the team?"

"You've observed the team this week. So, who do you want to give positive feedback to?"

Paul explained how he listened in on Harriet's call on Monday morning.

"Let's role play for a bit," said Jan. "What are you going to say to her? Same structure – what was the example, the impact, and the future action?"

Paul paused for a moment.

"Harriet. I listened in to some of your calls on Monday. You demonstrated some great objection handling and closing techniques. Do more of it."

"That's not bad. What specifically did Harriet do right?"

"She listened really well and asked the right questions."

Jan smiled.

"How do you know she listened well?"

"She didn't interrupt the customer, and she paused after they spoke. The questions she asked the customer were great at helping her to understand what the objections were. I thought that was brilliant."

"Well that's the specific feedback you need to give her. *That's* the behaviour you want her to repeat in the future."

Paul moved uncomfortably in his chair. He took a deep breath and sighed. "It seems very detailed."

"Yes it is. But the more specific the feedback, the more likely the person is to repeat the behaviour. Let's try it again."

Paul repeated it.

"Harriet. I listened in to some of your calls

on Monday. You demonstrated some fantastic objection handling and closing techniques. I really liked the fact that you listened. You didn't interrupt. You asked great questions to understand their issues and you used the techniques from the training course to overcome those objections. Harriet that was superb work. I'd love to see more of that."

Jan beamed from ear to ear.

"Great. What examples from this week have you got where someone's behaviour wasn't quite right?"

"Well, there was an instance with Izzy in our team meeting on Monday."

"Go on."

"She was a bit blunt with the team, and in particular with Harriet."

"Paul, pretend I'm Izzy for a minute. How would you give me feedback? Remember, be specific."

"Izzy, I want to speak to you about your behaviour in the team meeting on Monday. Harriet asked you a specific question regarding call volumes and you took a deep intake of breath and folded your arms before you started to speak. The answer you gave was short and incomplete. This said to the team that you were disinterested and not willing to participate in the meeting."

Paul paused and said to Jan "But if I say this to her, it's going to tick her off. She wants to leave, remember?"

Jan replied "Yes. I know that. You raise an interesting point. But first, what you've just said is really good. It was clear and focussed on specific behaviour. But remember, you must also focus on what *future* behaviour you want. In doing that, you may need to recognise the context of when you're giving feedback."

Paul looked at her quizzically.

"You need to acknowledge that you know she wants to leave, and you need to say that to her. You also need to tell her that you need her to perform while she's still here. So, once more from the top. Run Izzy's feedback by me again."

Paul shook himself. He was nearly there.

"Izzy, I want to speak to you about your behaviour in the team meeting on Monday. Harriet asked you a specific question regarding call volumes, you took a deep intake of breath and folded your arms before you started to speak. The answer you gave was short and incomplete. This said to me and the team that you were disinterested, and not willing to participate in the meeting. I know that your mind is elsewhere at the minute due to your uncertain future at *IVEX*, but I do need you to perform and participate at team meetings while you're still here."

Paul felt the train come to a slow halt. He was in Cardiff. His session with Jan had come to an end for another week.

Paul was excited about trying out feedback to improve his team's performance.

PAUL'S PAMBO PAD

FEEDBACK

Feedback is really about helping people change their future performance.

When I give feedback:

I should talk about specific examples and the Behaviour I have observed, the impact that behaviour is having and the actions I want from the team member in the future.

Performance = Ability x Motivation x Behaviour x Opportunity

15

The next day started with an enthused Paul making notes of his session with Jan on feedback.

He had to give positive feedback to Linda. He had to. She had held the team together for so many years, and Paul had taken her for granted.

As her colleague he never told her how much he loved working alongside her and how much he valued her contribution to the team. As her boss, it was his duty to tell her how much he valued her.

As usual, Linda came in to Paul's office just before 9am with a cup of tea. She placed it on his desk and before she turned away to leave Paul said "Linda, take a seat. I need to speak to you about something."

"Nothing too serious I hope?" said Linda, smiling as she took her seat.

"It is serious. It's something that should have been brought up a long time ago."

"What's the matter?"

"Nothing is the matter, Lind. I need to let you know that when you make a round of tea and coffee in the morning, you make everybody feel loved. You show that you care for the team, and I really value that. You bring in birthday cards, organise the presents, and our social functions. Without you this team would not have a heart. Please keep on doing what you're doing – I *really* appreciate it and so do the guys in the team."

Paul had never seen Linda so happy. She was moved, nearly to tears.

"Thank you. Thank you, Paul."

"It's no problem. It's been a long time coming."

Linda left the office, smiling and keen to get back to her desk.

"That felt better than any sales", thought Paul.

Now for the nasty bit. He had to speak to Izzy. He called her, and asked her to come in to his office, he could see she was between calls so she had no excuse. Izzy came in to the office, Paul thought back to his session with Jan…

After Paul finished giving Izzy the feedback, she said "You're right. There was no need to act the way I did. I'd had a bad weekend at home and didn't leave it at the door. It got to me and, because I'm unsure of my future at *IVEX*, I felt it was acceptable… and it's not."

Paul spoke with Izzy about her home issues, and they discussed each others' lives outside of *IVEX*, something they hadn't done since before Paul's promotion. Their chat had worked in more ways than one.

Paul immediately thought of H. He decided to give him a call. Paul spoke with H about Jan's model of feedback and how it had worked so well with Linda and Izzy.

"That sounds fantastic, Paul." said H. "How do you know when it is appropriate to give feedback?"

Paul didn't know the answer to that question.

"You would just give it to them, wouldn't you?" Paul's statement was just as much a guess as it was a question.

"Well, yes. Jan's model is very direct and adult. I guess what I'm getting at is that

115

feedback should follow without delay. You should try to give feedback as quickly as possible after observing the behaviour. But sometimes that might not be appropriate."

"I guess you're right. If there are customers or other members of the team around, you probably don't want to embarrass them. I guess I should just check that it's a good time to give feedback."

"Or perhaps we ask them for permission?" said H.

Paul agreed.

"Paul, why would you ask before you gave a member of your team feedback?"

"Sometimes it isn't appropriate. I guess you shouldn't give negative feedback if that person is about to head in to an important meeting, a vital sales pitch, or anything creative – I wouldn't want to wobble them."

H said "Yes. But who is the feedback of value to?"

"The team member?" Paul looked as if he was starting to understand where H was heading.

"Yes! So if you give feedback without permission, who holds the value?"

"The manager?"

"YES! We need to ensure the value of the feedback is with the receiver – not the giver. It needs to be of value to the team member, not a release for the manager."

"So how do I ask for permission?"

H paused for a second.

"I guess I would ask them if they had a moment. I would say that I wanted to chat to them. Or, if I wanted to be more direct, I would say 'can I give you some feedback?' As a manager you need to make the call depending on the severity of the issue."

Paul agreed. That made sense to him. He could see the importance of asking for permission and checking it was the right time.

Paul put down the phone, smiled and thought of all the times that H had given him feedback in the past… and that he had used exactly that model.

H truly was a great manager.

16

Monday morning came. Paul had an enjoyable weekend visiting family. He felt refreshed and energised, ready to tackle the week.

Unfortunately, it didn't take long for a problem to arise. It was 9:00am and there was no sign of Dylan. This was the first time Paul was pleased at a member of his staff being late. This was the perfect opportunity to give Dylan feedback on his time keeping.

As Dylan strolled in at 9:08am, Paul calmly walked over and placed a hand on his shoulder. Dylan took the headphones out of his ears.

"Morning." mumbled Dylan.

"Morning Dylan, can you come into my office please?"

He seemed to notice Paul's seriousness.

As Dylan entered Paul's office and sat down, Paul made the decision not to ask for permission to give feedback. It was too serious an issue. Dylan had pushed him too far.

"Dylan, when you turn up nearly ten minutes late it sends a message to the rest of the team that it is acceptable. It also sends a message to me that you don't respect me. You know I have spoken to you previously about this, and you're still doing it."

Paul was confident that he gotten through to Dylan, but he wasn't done there.

"What's the story? Why are you regularly late?" asked Paul.

Dylan replied "My bus sometimes gets caught in traffic, so it delays me five or ten minutes."

"Dyl, what time does your bus leave your stop?"

"8:15am"

"Right, is there an earlier bus?" probed Paul.

"There's one at 8:00am."

"Right," said Paul. "What do you think is the best thing to do?"

"Get the earlier bus?" asked Dylan.

Paul nodded.

"So we're clear. I expect you to be in by 9:00am every morning."

He nodded, turned and left the room. Dylan knew things were changing around *IVEX*.

Paul was becoming a good manager.

FEEDBACK

Focus on specific behaviours, their impact and what actions you want to see in the future...

• be direct and adult about giving feedback

• feedback should follow without delay. You should try to give feedback as quickly as possible after observing the behaviour.
But sometimes that might not be appropriate

• feedback should be of value to the receiver. It needs to be of value to the team member not just a release for me

• depending on the severity, check that it is a good time to give feedback. Sometimes it might be a wrong time for the individual to get feedback.

Performance = Ability x Motivation x Behaviour x Opportunity

17

A few weeks went by and Paul made sure he spoke with his team and held one to one sessions regularly. They would talk about issues and work through any problems that came up. He gave them praise when they were doing something well and pulled them up on things that needed improving.

Paul felt as if bridges were being built, progress was being made and performance was improving. He was beginning to see how useful PAMBO was in helping him improve his team's performance.

The feedback he had given to Dylan had clearly worked. Dylan turned up on time now.

Brandenberg, the MD, was pleased with Paul. He was happy with sales and Paul's performance as manager. In fact, they were both pleased with how things were going.

A conversation with Harriet that week had made Paul realise that he needed to change something. He learnt that sometimes he got things wrong.

In a one to one with Harriet, it came out that during team meetings Paul would always ask her opinion last. He would go to Izzy first, then Linda, then Dylan and lastly Harriet. Harriet told Paul that when she was left until last this made her feel annoyed and undervalued in the team.

Paul felt awful.

He had apologised and assured Harriet he would include her more often.

Paul hadn't met with Jan for a couple of weeks as she had been away on holiday. Initially, he was concerned about missing their weekly sessions. However, upon reflection, the fortnight break allowed him to work on embedding the new skills and knowledge he had gained from their previous conversations.

Paul looked forward to his sessions with Jan, and was excited as he had much to tell her since they met last.

"Tell me about the past couple of weeks.

How did you get on with giving the team feedback?" asked Jan.

Paul explained his feedback and the improvement in Dylan's timekeeping.

Jan was pleased "Great. Sounds like you're getting the hang of feedback."

"Paul, I think it's time we talked about opportunity. It completes PAMBO in its' simplest form. What do you think I mean by opportunity?"

"I'm really not sure, is it what I can provide for my team?"

"Yes! Opportunity is what the company provides, and what you do as their manager to help them to do a good job. You have to give them the opportunity to use their ability and motivation to do their job properly. What does *IVEX* provide you with, to do *your* job properly?"

"Well, an office for one." laughed Paul.

Jan smiled.

"What does *IVEX* have to provide the team with for them to do their job?"

"They have to give us computers, telephones, initial training, desks and I guess they give us performance reviews."

Paul was surprised with his own answers. Of course, there had to be opportunity. Without the resources and management support there was no way Paul's team were going to perform well.

"So, Paul" asked Jan "what else do you have to give your team in order for them to perform?"

Paul looked into Jan's eyes.

"If they need support I'm there for them. I think I've learned that now."

"You're really getting it." beamed Jan. "What do you think your team will feel if you provide them with the right opportunities?"

"Valued. They'll feel loved. They'll feel like they're important and are more likely to do a better job."

"You've got it. So how would you make sure that you are giving them the opportunities they need?"

"I guess I could ask them if there is anything else I can do to help them do their job better."

Jan smiled.

"That's a great point Paul. Every opportunity you get you need to ask them if you can help them. Team meetings and one to one sessions – they're all there for you to provide your team with the opportunity to do a good job."

"So, of all the stuff you've learned, what's the thing that's had the greatest impact on your team?" said Jan.

Paul was slightly taken aback by the change in direction.

"Feedback. Regular feedback."

Paul had realised that feedback was the management tool that helped his team improve their ability, maintain their motivation, and demonstrate the right behaviours. It was the management practice that helped performance improve.

Jan nodded. "Yep. If you combine feedback with the appropriate management style you're on to a winner."

"Style?" asked Paul.

"Yes. You need to develop your management style. You need to learn how to deal with people according to their needs. Your management style and resources are the two facets of opportunity. The style is about how you manage people and how you develop somebody's performance. If somebody is new at a job you would manage them differently than if they were experienced in the role. On the first day of the job a new starter will want to do a good job."

That last sentence struck a chord with Paul.

Jan leaned in. "Your job is to make them feel as though they want to do a good job every day".

Paul nodded. *"What a great way to put it,"* he thought.

"But Paul, we're getting a little ahead of ourselves. Management style is a whole other issue."

As Paul was leaving the train he got a call from H. He hadn't spoken with him for a while. They had a brief catch up regarding a few issues. H had been away. He regularly visited the south of France. He owned a villa and visited it at least twice a year with his wife. Talking with H about his holiday made him realise that he had forgotten to ask Jan how her trip was. He felt awful.

Paul spoke with H about his one to one sessions and feedback and the positive effect it was having on the team.

"You've got to remember that you're there to help the team Paul. You may be their boss but one of your key roles is helping them do a good job. You must be clear about objectives and expectations so they know what good performance looks like. And feedback is a great way to enforce the behaviours you expect to see."

OPPORTUNITY

The final part of PAMBO is opportunity. This is about the resources the organisation provides to help people do a great job and it is about my management style.

How I manage people on a day to day basis:

the feedback I give them,

the opportunities I give them to contribute and improve performance.

I guess people want

to do a good job

and my job is not

to get in the way

of that happening...

Performance = Ability x Motivation x Behaviour x Opportunity

18

Paul desperately wanted Izzy to realise that the *Connect* role was not the right move for her.

He walked over to her desk that Thursday afternoon. Izzy and Harriet had been discussing an issue regarding a demanding client. It was great to see Izzy passing her experience and knowledge on.

"Iz, can I see you in my office for a moment?"

"No problem" came the reply.

As she joined Paul in his office, he noticed that she appeared to be guarded. Her body language suggested that she was in no mood to talk about anything other than why she was in his office.

Paul got straight to the point.

"Iz, we need to talk about *Connect*. I don't think they're the right firm for you."

There followed an incredibly uncomfortable silence.

"No Paul. My mind is made up. In a few weeks I'll have a fresh start. It's what I need after years of this place. I've become stale. I take issues home with me these days that shouldn't be issues at all."

"Iz, you're not wrong, and I agree that you need to further progress in your career. I just don't think it's with *Connect*. It's a bigger commute for you and they have a huge turnover in staff and, let's be honest, a poor reputation."

She looked at the ceiling in a bid to avoid any further tension.

"I need to leave, Paul. I know *Connect* isn't the ideal move for me but it's my only option."

"No it's not! Why leave for a firm that is four times the size of *IVEX*? You're not likely to get much development and you're just another cog in the wheel."

"You don't know that! You've never worked there so how can you comment on *Connect*?"

"Oh come on Iz! You've heard all the same

stories I have."

Izzy squirmed uncomfortably in her chair.

Paul was right.

However, Izzy's mind was made up and she was leaving.

That was final.

Paul then felt something he hadn't felt in the best part of a year. Izzy's hand on his own. He looked into her eyes as she spoke.

"Paul, as a friend, you need to get someone in the team now. You need to recruit an experienced body, maybe two, and you need to spend time with them. You've started to do some really good stuff these past few weeks and you need to keep it up."

She looked at Paul with her chin held high.

"Paul, I have loved working with you for the majority of our time together and I look forward to rekindling our friendship once I start my new job."

Izzy rose from her chair and placed a letter on Paul's desk. She stopped, gave him a wry smile, and made her way to the door and left the office. Paul, eyes fixed on Izzy as she walked back to her desk, grabbed the letter.

It was her notice.

In one month, Izzy would be gone.

Paul looked over Izzy's letter. It hit him in a second wave. He was going to lose his closest colleague. Someone he had cared for and worked with for nearly his entire professional career.

Paul's mobile rang. It was H. He was sure H had a secret camera on him. He always seemed to call when Paul needed him most.

"Hi H!"

"Paul, whatever you're doing, stop and get in your office. We need to talk."

"I'm in my office. Go for it."

"I'm staying in Cambridge permanently. Things have picked up in a big way since the restructure and Brandenberg is adamant that we shouldn't stifle momentum."

"What does that mean?"

"It means that he is impressed with you and the newly created role. He wants to replicate it over here. We're appointing a new Sales Team Manager for the East – and we want it to be Izzy."

Paul couldn't believe it.

"I'm calling to let you know that I will be contacting Izzy by the end of the day to offer her the position. She was very close to getting the promotion that you got. Brandenberg and I think she's ready for a good move and we don't want to lose her."

It certainly was a bittersweet emotion for Paul. On the one hand he was delighted that his dear friend was to be promoted and given a whole new lease of life. But on the other hand he was to lose Izzy and H on a permanent basis.

Paul's feelings aside, it was the perfect solution.

He had to accept that.

H spoke with Paul for a short while, reassuring him that Izzy would be looked after properly should she choose to accept.

He knew this was the right choice for Izzy. He hoped that she accepted the position, and turned down the offer from *Connect*. There really was no comparison.

It was just after 3pm, the time when he knew H's call had been made. Izzy burst in to Paul's office with a smile that had evaded Paul for months.

She didn't even have to say anything.

He knew she had accepted.

He gave her a hug and they laughed. A few tears were shed, but they were happy ones. Paul felt a huge weight come off his shoulders. He was so utterly relieved that he had his friend back.

They decided not to communicate the news to the rest of the team until it was official and the paperwork had been signed.

The rest of the afternoon was a write-off for Paul. He couldn't concentrate on anything, and neither could Izzy.

Paul left the office at 5pm and made his way to Bristol Temple Meads station. His train arrived on time and he walked on with a smile on his face.

To his confusion, Jan was on the train.

He immediately hurried over.

"It's Thursday! What are you doing on here? Is everything ok?"

"Everything is fine Paul. I had to go into the Bristol office today."

"How come?"

"Well, nobody else is going to collect my things, are they?"

"What!?" cried Paul.

Jan laughed.

"I'm leaving. I'm moving away. My husband has just been permanently relocated."

"Where to?" asked Paul.

"Cambridge."

"That's bizarre. My boss has just been permanently relocated to Cambridge."

Paul detected Jan's wry smile. "Hang on, what does your husband do?"

Jan's smile grew bigger.

Paul stopped her before she replied.

"Actually, what is your husband's name?!"

"Harry. Harry Jacobs."

"H!?"

"Some people call him that. I prefer Harry."

"But H's wife is called JJ!"

Jan pursed her lips.

"Jan... Jacobs..." said Paul as the penny dropped.

"You've known all along who I am!? You've known my story all along?'

Paul couldn't believe it.

"I feel cheated!" But Paul was only half serious. He really wasn't sure if he was annoyed or not.

"Paul. We wouldn't have been able to achieve what we have if you had known who I was."

"I'm not disagreeing… but come on!"

Jan chuckled to herself.

"Did you never work it out, Paul? All the evidence was there. JJ. Jan Jacobs. The fact Harry and I both went away at the same time. His acceptance that you were being coached by an exterior party. Would a manager instantly accept that you are being coached by someone completely unconnected with the business?"

Paul couldn't believe it. She was right. How blind was he not to see the obvious. Jan reassuringly touched him on the arm.

"Paul, forget about it. You've started to achieve what we set out to do. You're on your way to becoming a very effective manager. PAMBO will help you maximise the performance of your team – but only if you stay disciplined and committed to developing them."

Paul looked out of the window.

He realised that he was only at the beginning of the journey.

Jan smiled. "Paul, remember what you've learned. I would love to help you when you get Izzy's replacement on board. Keep in touch."

Michael Baker

Working with the highest calibre of clients across the private, public, and third sector has given Michael a valuable insight into different work cultures. A proud Irishman, his extensive experience in the engineering, financial services, hospitality and manufacturing industries has helped many businesses and organisations grow successful leaders and managers. An MBA graduate of the *University of Bath*, Michael believes that although leadership is hugely important, the basics of encouraging good performance lie in people management, and so he researched and developed the PAMBO model.

James Davies

James never dreamt of running a PR agency or becoming a published author, but that's life for you! After an extensive learning experience at Swansea University, James held a number of jobs in the PR industry until he decided to strike out for himself and founded *Compass Media Relations*. A few years of hard work later, he finds himself with a breadth of experience in delivering communications and press coverage for businesses across a wide array of sectors. On his involvement with PAMBO, James says: "PAMBO has not only been a fantastic project to work on – it has been a great learning experience that has made me a better writer, and a better manager."

THE TBC

Since 2002, *The Training and Business Consultancy Ltd (the TBC)* has been at the forefront of management training and leadership development. Over the years, its varied catalogue of clients has benefited from the experience and knowledge of some of the best business psychologists and leadership consultants in their fields.

The company's mission is simple: *"To improve the performance of individuals, teams, and organisations."* The team achieves this by spending time with businesses in order to fully understand their specific needs, then by engaging with them on personalised training programme. Every programme is designed with one goal in mind – to turn good managers into great ones.

If you want to chat to the team at the TBC about how we can help you, or your team, to manage people better then please get in touch:

theTBC.com

info@thetbc.com